Ancient Greek Homes

Haydn Middleton

Heinemann
LIBRARY

www.heinemann.co.uk/library
Visit our website to find out more information about **Heinemann Library** books.

To order:
 Phone 44 (0) 1865 888066
 Send a fax to 44 (0) 1865 314091
 Visit the Heinemann Bookshop at www.heinemann.co.uk/library to browse our catalogue and order online.

First published in Great Britain by Heinemann Library, Halley Court, Jordan Hill, Oxford OX2 8EJ, a division of Reed Educational and Professional Publishing Ltd. Heinemann is a registered trademark of Reed Educational & Professional Publishing Limited.

OXFORD MELBOURNE AUCKLAND JOHANNESBURG BLANTYRE
GABORONE IBADAN PORTSMOUTH NH (USA) CHICAGO

Designed by Tinstar Design (www.tinstar.co.uk)
Illustrations by Jeff Edwards, Art Construction and Martin Smillie.
Originated by Ambassador Litho Ltd.
Printed by Wing King Tong in Hong Kong.

ISBN 0 431 14541 5   (hardback)   ISBN 0 431 14546 6   (paperback)
06 05 04 03 02   07 06 05 04 03
10 9 8 7 6 5 4 3 2 1   10 9 8 7 6 5 4 3 2 1

British Library Cataloguing in Publication Data
Middleton, Haydn
       Ancient Greek homes. – (People in the past)
       1. Dwellings – Greece – History – To 1500 – Juvenile literature
       2. Greece – Social conditions – To 146 B.C. – Juvenile literature
       3. Greece – Civilization – To 146 B.C. – Juvenile literature
       I.Title
       640.9'38

Acknowledgements
The Publishers would like to thank the following for permission to reproduce photographs:
AKG London pp13, 14, 22, 26, 28, 31, 36, 37, Ancient Art and Architecture Collection pp6, 7, 11, 24, 27, 32, 39, 40, Ashmolean Museum p30, British Museum p18, CM Dixon pp8, 35, Corbis pp12, 21, 34, Michael Holford pp10, 38.

Cover photograph reproduced with permission of AKG (Erich Lessing).

Every effort has been made to contact copyright holders of any material reproduced in this book. Any omissions will be rectified in subsequent printings if notice is given to the Publisher.

The Publishers would like to thank Dr Michael Vickers of the Ashmolean Museum, Oxford, for his assistance in the preparation of this book.

Words appearing in the text in bold, **like this**, are explained in the glossary.

Contents

The ancient-Greek world

When people talk about ancient Greece, they do not just mean the modern-day country of Greece as it used to be. The ancient-Greek world was made up of the hot, rocky mainland of Greece, plus hundreds of islands in the Aegean, Ionian and Adriatic Seas, with further overseas settlements in places ranging from northern Africa to what we now call Turkey and Italy. The earliest Greek-speakers did not think they all belonged to a single country. For a long while they did not even think they all belonged to the same **civilization**.

For centuries the mightiest people in the Greek world were the Minoans, based on the island of Crete. Power then passed to the warlike Mycenaeans, based on the mainland region known as the **Peloponnese**. This was followed around the year 1100 BC by centuries of confusion and upheaval.

In the later 'Classical Age', from about 500 BC until about 300 BC, prosperity was restored by the rise of many city-states like Athens and Sparta. The Greek word for city-state was *polis*. Each *polis* controlled the villages and farmland around it.

Vanishing houses

Daily life varied from place to place in the widespread ancient-Greek world, and so – probably – did the homes that people lived in. Very few houses have survived. We can still see many ruins of great Greek temples and other public buildings because these were built to last, out of stone and marble. Most private houses on the other hand were made of less permanent materials like sun-dried mud bricks. Even if a larger house had floors of stone, after the house fell empty people would often take away the stone to use on other buildings. So little of it now exists for **archaeologists** to examine.

However, from ancient books as well as from archaeological remains, there is enough evidence to piece together what Greek homes were like. This evidence also gives us a glimpse of the men, women and children who lived in them over two thousand years ago.

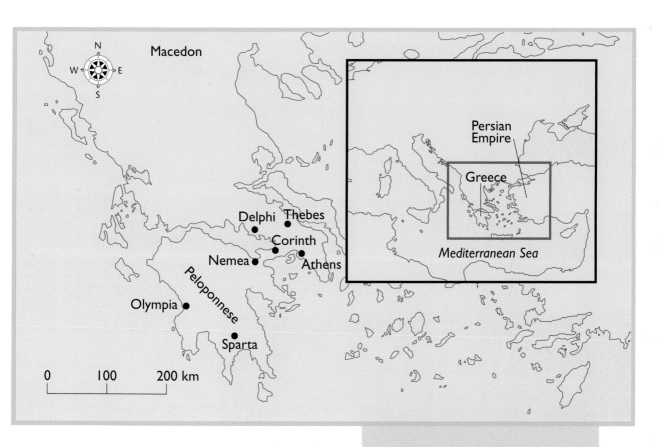

Ancient Greece was not a single unified country but a collection of many separate states that varied greatly in size and strength. The ancient Greeks used the word *Hellas* to mean all the places where there was a Greek way of life.

The family unit

Ancient-Greek life was run largely by men, and largely for the benefit of men. They did all the top public jobs and had far more legal rights than their womenfolk. The basic unit of Greek **society**, from the richest to the poorest, was the family – and within the family, women held a vital position. In some family homes three generations lived under a single roof: grandparents, a married son and his wife, and their children. In larger homes there might even be more relatives – unmarried, widowed or sometimes divorced. The head of such a household was always a man, but the task of making it run smoothly fell to women – whether they were members of the family, maidservants or slaves.

Servants of the state

'It is a crime,' the **philosopher** Plato wrote, 'to refuse to take a wife.' Greek men were fully expected to marry by the age of 35. In Sparta, a confirmed bachelor could have all his rights as a **citizen** taken away from him. The families of the bride and groom often arranged marriages and these were **economic** unions rather than love matches. By merging the fortunes of two families, more wealth could be created for the *polis*.

A bride and groom on their wedding procession. Brides brought gifts called 'dowries' to their new husbands. The richer a girl's family, the greater the gift might be. It could be as much as ten per cent of her father's wealth or property.

A Greek woman serving a man. Greek women had far fewer rights than most women today. They were seldom supposed to leave the home, let alone do jobs or have a say in the way that the *polis* was governed.

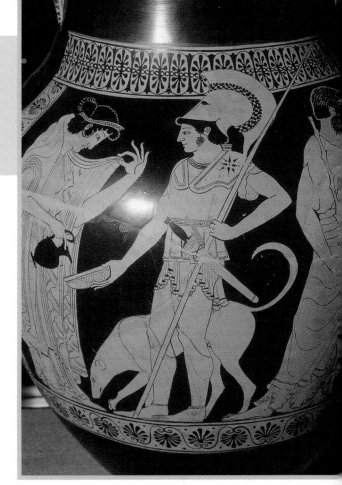

Meanwhile, any sons could one day fight to protect the state during the many wars and any daughters could in turn give birth to future heads of the household. All children had to look after their elderly parents, then honour them too after they died – by leaving offerings of food or drink at their graves and tying coloured ribbons around their tombstones.

Even states as large as Athens had no regular police forces. So governments relied heavily on the head of each family to make sure that all the members of his household – including any servants and slaves – obeyed the law. In that way, his home was like a city-state in miniature, with him as its ruler.

The Spartan exception

The family unit in Sparta was organized on unusual lines. There, the state government – not heads of families – laid down strict rules for everyone. Boys were sent away from home aged seven, to live together in army **barracks** and train to be full-time soldiers. After the age of 30 they might take wives and live in normal homes, but even then they were often away on military campaigns for months on end. This meant that Spartan women had more independence in managing their households. Unlike women elsewhere in Greece, they could even own land and property, and make decisions on what to do with it.

The *oikos*

The Greek word for a home was *oikos*. As well as meaning the house's brick, stone or clay baked by the sun (most Greek homes were very simply made) it also meant the family that lived inside it or the 'household'. It could also mean a wealthy family's **estate**. In this sense, the modern historian J.K. Davies has defined the *oikos* as 'a machine for drawing an income from'.

Family fortunes

In Athens, such estates did not pass as a whole from father to son. They were often split apart on the owner's death among his surviving **heirs**. Depending on how careful the new owners were, great fortunes could be lost or made quite quickly.

The seated figure here is Zeus – head of the household of Greek gods and goddesses on Mount Olympus.

At the start of the great-thinker Plato's book *The Republic*, a wealthy **metic** called Cephalus said: 'As a money-maker I hold a place somewhere between my grandfather and my father. For my grandfather inherited about as much as I now possess and multiplied it many times, my father Lysanias reduced it below the present amount, and I'll be happy if I shall leave to these boys a little more and no less than I inherited.'

An *oikos* could be ruined if the head of the household frittered away family money through gambling, breeding racehorses, or domestic entertainment. In the 420s BC a man called Kallias inherited so much money that he was thought to be the richest man in Greece. Within 40 years, his extravagance had helped to reduce the family property worth over 1,200,000 **drachmas** to less than 12,000 *drachmas*. By comparison, many manual workers earned just one *drachma* a day.

In the course of five generations, only one family in Classical Athens was always in the wealthiest class. Meanwhile 357 other families seemed to pass from rags to riches and back to rags in just one generation. It is worth remembering what an unstable world the ancient Greeks lived in, as we now look at the kinds of homes they inhabited.

Human tools

Historians used to believe that most Athenian households had at least one domestic slave. However, slaves would have been expensive to buy and also to feed, so maybe they were not quite so common. Even so, in 5th-century BC Athens there were between eighty and a hundred thousand slaves. That was one slave for every free member of the population. Most of them were foreign – **Persians** or Asians captured during warfare; some were the children of slave-parents.

Slaves in Sparta, Thessaly or Sicily often led hard lives, but Athenian slaves could sometimes be mistaken for regular members of a family. It made sense for families to treat their slaves with some

consideration. The writer Aristotle described them as 'human tools' – and only an idiot would mistreat his own tools. Some slaves could eventually buy their own freedom and go on – like the ex-slave banker Pasion – to become highly successful businessmen.

This bronze statuette shows an African who was captured and made to serve as a slave in ancient Greece. Most slaves came from Asia and the Middle East.

Master-slave relations

Greek authors referred to household slaves performing various specific tasks: females assisted with childcare, while male slaves might work in the kitchen or answer the door to visitors. Their behaviour was not always very

Women drawing water from a well. Female slaves were more often seen in public like this than rich women. They might also work outside the home as cooks, cleaners, nannies, grape-pickers or barmaids.

servile. In the book *Protagoras* by the great thinker and writer Plato, a bad-tempered slave at the house of Kallias slammed the door in the face of the **philosopher** Socrates. It is probable that masters punished their slaves with beatings and even tortured them. Yet some close relationships were formed. According to the Athenian writer Xenophon in his *Memoirs of Socrates*: if a slave died, men were more likely to grieve over him than at the death of a friend.

It does not seem that slaves had their own separate **quarters** in either town or country houses. Xenophon mentioned a house where the male slaves slept in the *andron*, or men's part of the house, and female slaves in the *gunaikon* or women's part. Since slaves lived so intimately with the free, it is easy to understand why a character in Euripides' play *Helen* says: 'It is bad not to feel with your masters, laugh with them, and sympathize in their sorrows.'

Building materials

◁▷ ◁▷ ◁▷ ◁▷ ◁▷ ◁▷ ◁▷ ◁▷ ◁▷ ◁▷ ◁▷ ◁▷ ◁▷ ◁▷ ◁▷ ◁▷ ◁▷ ◁▷

Ancient-Greek public buildings – like temples, theatres and law-courts – were built to last, out of stone or marble. The ruins of many of them can still be seen today, after more than two thousand years. However the Greeks, unlike the Romans in later centuries, seemed less interested in building very grand homes for themselves. This was partly because the hot and dry Greek climate made it possible to spend a great deal of time out of doors, rather than cooped up inside.

In both the city and country, most ordinary houses from 500 to 300 BC were made of sunbaked bricks on a stone foundation, with floors of beaten earth, roofs covered in thatch or tiles made of clay and small windows with wooden shutters but no glass. These were far less permanent structures than the public buildings. Burglars were known as 'wall-piercers'. If walls could be 'pierced', this suggests that they cannot have been very solid.

There is even less evidence of basic Greek home-furnishings. Wooden chests, couches, chairs, stools and tables tend to disintegrate over the centuries, so we must examine ancient images to see how they might once have looked. Fortunately, some floors made of pebble-**mosaic** have been found.

This image of a seated woman opening a box dates from the 5th century BC. The interior furnishings look quite ornate, but most homes probably had little external decoration.

Piecing the past together

Houses have been **excavated** on sites all over the Greek world. In cities they seem to have been packed closely together in blocks. Most of the walls and roofs have long since vanished – leaving only the base of the stone foundations. From these, it is often hard to tell even where the entrances to different rooms might have been. **Archaeologists** have worked out that some houses had an upper storey, after finding stone bases that would once have supported wooden staircases.

Archaeologists often also find at house-sites pottery fragments, objects made out of stone or metal and coins. If pieces of plates are found in a certain area, that may mean that once it was a dining room. Or it could simply mean that this was the part of the house where broken crockery was dumped!

The coming of concrete

Southern Italy and Sicily were part of the **Hellenistic** world and from Italy, in the late 3rd century BC, a new building technique began to appear – construction in concrete. In time, concrete became the best material for building **vaults** in more elaborate buildings. It was cheap and strong, damp-resistant and fireproof, and on big projects it could easily be used by unskilled labourers who were sometimes slaves or prisoners-of-war. Early concrete buildings were faced with carefully fitted pieces of rubble. Some were even developed into ancient kinds of high-rise **tenement** blocks.

This picture of a young woman, admiring herself in a hand mirror, comes from a vase painting of about 430 BC. Behind her is an open door showing a bedroom beyond.

Different kinds of homes

Family houses everywhere were often built from similar materials – but they differed depending on which part of the Greek or **Hellenistic** world they stood in and on when exactly they were built. They also differed according to how much money was spent on them, and in the personal tastes of their owners. From writings and archaeological remains we have more evidence of larger, more lavish homes than of smaller ones, which were usually made of perishable materials.

Many Greek houses did have common features. In the 5th, 4th and 3rd centuries BC, most were built around an open courtyard with a **portico** along at least one side. Many household jobs were done in this courtyard, which might contain a well, while a number of rooms would lead off it – where visitors were entertained. One room might be a small shop, with its own street entrance. Then there would be some bedrooms and storerooms. Writers mentioned houses that had their own gyms and bathrooms – but these must have been unusual.

The courtyard of the House of the Dionysus on Delos, dating from the late second century BC. A cistern beneath it provided this house's water-supply.

Hellenistic houses

From Hellenistic times we have evidence of striking new homes that were built for wealthy officials and merchants and their families. These high-quality houses in cities like Priene and Delos usually focused on a small courtyard, and had at least one big reception room that often opened from the north side of a **peristyle**, so that it could catch the sun in winter. The surfaces inside were protected – and made attractive – by mosaic pavements and painted **stucco** wall-decorations. There might also have been statues or marble furnishings set in the **colonnades**. You can see the ruins of one of them in the picture.

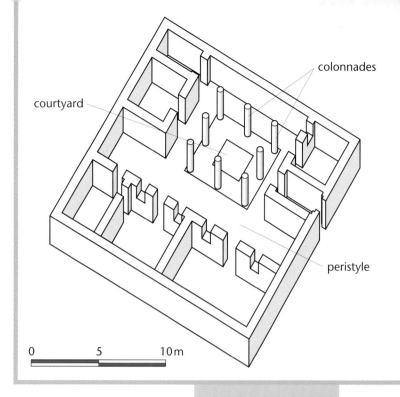

courtyard

colonnades

peristyle

0   5   10 m

A reconstruction drawing of what a peristyle house in Delos would have looked like.

Sizeable inner space

Some Greek houses were far bigger than others. Kallias was one of the richest men in Athens. The courtyard of his home had two colonnades around it – each one so wide that a number of men were able to walk side-by-side and talk within it. We know that from this description in Plato's *Protagoras*: 'When we entered the house, we found Protagoras walking about in the portico, and walking around with him in a line were on one side Kallias, son of Hipponikos and his half-brother Paralos, the son of Pericles, and Charmides, the son of Glaukon; on the other side were Pericles' other son, Xanthippos and Philippides, son of Philomelos, and Antimoiros of Mende.' Behind them were even more people, listening-in to their fascinating conversation.

Homes in the city

In modern Greece many towns and cities now stand on the sites of ancient cities. This makes it hard for **archaeologists** to gain access to the remains of older buildings. (Sometimes there are no remains at all – since any hardwearing material like stone has been used for later buildings.) As a result, we cannot be sure how most Greek cities were planned, or what the homes in them were like.

However, in 1928 archaeological work began at a site on the Chalkidiki peninsula in northern Greece. There at Olynthos, three thousand years ago, a city grew up with residential areas which by the end of the 5th century BC spread over two flat-topped hills. The politician Demosthenes recorded that in 348 BC, the army of Philip II of Macedon destroyed the city and enslaved any surviving inhabitants. No one ever lived on the site again, so the archaeologists who excavated at Olynthos until 1938 were given a rare glimpse of just how an ancient city was laid out. They explored more than a hundred houses – and what they found is a vital source of information on Greek homes.

Archaeologists and historians use great ingenuity to work out what ancient-Greek houses might once have looked like. This is a suggestion of how one of the larger houses at Olynthos looked.

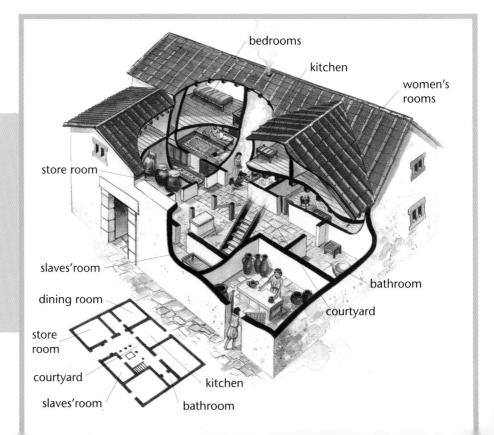

bedrooms

kitchen

women's rooms

store room

slaves' room

bathroom

dining room

courtyard

store room

courtyard

slaves' room

kitchen

bathroom

City blocks

Many of the houses at Olynthos formed blocks of a standard size. Each block consisted of two rows of houses, with each row sharing **party walls**. Each row had enough space for five houses measuring roughly 17x17 square metres – 290 square metres in all. (Measure the length and width of your own home to see how it compares). The two rows of houses were separated by a *stenopos*, a narrow alley for drainage. The mudbrick walls and tiled roofs had almost entirely disappeared, so it was hard for the archaeologists to tell if the houses had one storey or two. The vast majority of homes had just one entrance, at the front, but next to the pedestrian door some had a double-door used by carts delivering, for example, grain or items of furniture. These doorways were normally on the house's north or south-facing side.

Seen from above, a standard city block at Olynthos would have looked like this plan.

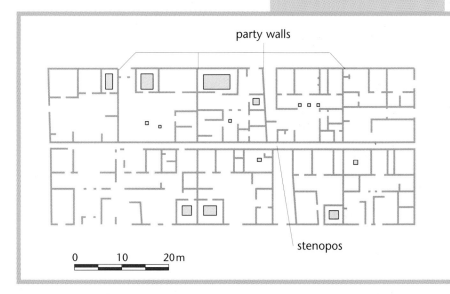

party walls

stenopos

0   10   20m

Light on the matter

Some house walls at other city archaeological sites are better preserved than those found at Olynthos. In these, any ground-floor windows that faced the street seem to have been small in size and high up in the walls. Not much light would have come in through them – but these small, high openings may also have been important for **ventilation**. Although city-house interiors were probably quite dark, there may have been low windows or doorways that looked out on a lighter inner courtyard.

Homes of the rich

From archaeological remains, it is not always easy to tell which ancient houses belonged to rich people. It would seem natural for richer families to live in bigger homes, but as the politician Demosthenes pointed out, the houses of Athens' leading statesmen used to look very similar to those of lesser citizens. Some houses, like that of the wealthy Kallias, were obviously enormous. If a house had a bathroom or damp-excluding plaster on its walls and mosaics on its floors, it probably belonged to a well-off family.

With lots of slaves and servants in the household, however, the owners still might not have had much space to themselves.

This vase painting shows Greek women – probably from wealthy backgrounds – holding up domestic utensils. Note, too, the elegant chair that can just be made out on the right of the painting.

A lack of luxury goods

Another way for **archaeologists** to tell if rich people lived in a particular house is by examining the objects found on the site. Again, one would expect rich people to have left behind some precious personal items. Unfortunately wooden articles could have rotted away over time and although metal goods are less perishable, they may have been taken away long ago because of their value.

Interestingly, it seems that Greek people did not share our modern tendency to invest money in **consumer durables**. 'When someone has enough furniture for his house,' wrote Xenophon, 'he stops buying it there and then.' He added that no man had yet had so much silver that he did not want more of it. This suggests that they were interested in showing off their wealth with expensive **status symbols**. Also they had no need for pricey labour-saving devices – since they had slaves to do all the time-consuming chores!

Paintings show us the sparse way in which rich people furnished and decorated their homes. The teacher and writer Theophrastus mocked a greedy, ambitious man not only for having a luxurious house – but also a pet monkey, a short-tailed ape, Sicilian doves, Laconian dogs, a jackdaw, dice made from gazelle horn, walking sticks from Sparta and a **Persian** carpet. Obviously, this man had gone too far but we know very little about the luxury items owned by other wealthy Athenians.

Modest belongings

In 415 BC around fifty Athenians, most of them wealthy, were found guilty of vandalizing statues. Their goods were all sold off in an auction and **inscriptions** survive recording details of the sale. There we can read how much land and how many valuable homes and slaves the guilty men owned – yet their personal goods amounted to little more than a pile of bronze pots, kitchen utensils and tunics. Their cash or any items made from precious metals would have gone straight into the Treasury of the city-state.

Homes in the country

In ancient-Greek documents the words *aulion* and *epaulis* were used to describe houses outside the cities. What they signified varied widely from place to place. Sometimes they meant a country farmhouse or even a kind of palace. At other times they meant just an animal shelter. You might think that country farmhouses would be very different from **urban** dwellings. In fact, they seem to have been built along much the same lines. This was possibly because most households everywhere depended on agricultural produce for their survival. So a similar range of facilities, like storerooms, would have been required.

Fixtures and fittings?

Nowadays when people move out of a house, they usually leave behind certain 'fixtures and fittings'. This does not seem to have been so in ancient Greece. The historian Thucydides wrote that when people fled from the countryside around Athens during the **Peloponnesian** War, they took some wooden architectural fittings from their farm buildings with them. Other documents show that houses were rented out sometimes without doors; and when houses were sold, doors were listed as part of the furniture and therefore not part of the sale. In this curious way, you could make your next home reminiscent of the one before!

An excavated house at Vari was laid out like this. On the next page you can find out what each of the inner spaces might have been used for.

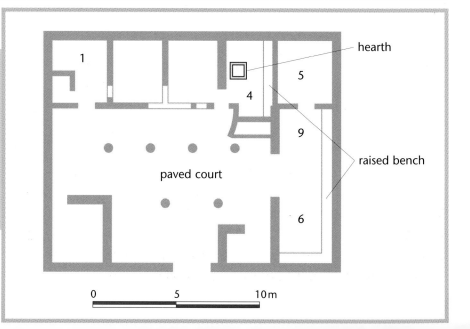

20

The Attica countryside, near Vari, looks like this today.

Evidence from Vari

Excavations at Vari, in Attica, have given us a good idea of what a big country house looked like towards the end of the 4th century BC (see diagram on page 20). This one covered a ground area of about 13 x 18 metres squared, including a large paved courtyard at the building's centre and south. The house's single entrance led directly into this courtyard, while a **portico** probably once sheltered the entrances to the rooms on its north and east sides. In room 1 there were traces of burning, so a cooking hearth or **brazier** may have been located here. In room 4 and again in rooms 6 and 9 – which run into each other – a stone bench along the wall may have been used as a base for seats or couches.

The most secluded and therefore most private part in the house seems to have been room 5. The **archaeologists** found no evidence to suggest what went on in this room. It may have had no special function at all – in city and country houses alike, rooms often served a variety of different purposes for different members of the household. Finally, room 7 was built on very solid foundations – perhaps because it was the base of a two-storey tower or *pyrgos*. We know that country houses elsewhere sometimes had such towers. Perhaps they were used as look-out points in times of war. Parts of them have remained, although the houses they once belonged to have disappeared.

Homes of the poor

It can be hard to decide if an **excavated** house once belonged to a poor family. According to ancient-Greek writers, several poor families might all live under the same roof, but archaeological remains cannot tell us how many people lived in any house. It is unlikely too, since the dwellings of the very poorest people were probably made of cheap materials, that they would have survived.

Poor households at Olynthos?

The excavators at Olynthos in northern Greece found a range of homes. Some of them were very small, with no traces of decoration, and they had very little privacy. Just inside their front doors, it would have been possible to look into the entire interior. This made it hard to separate any women's **quarters** from men's quarters – unless curtains or wooden partitions were used to mark

The country-worker at the plough being drawn by these oxen could have been a 'peasant' or small farmer.

off spaces inside. Yet the rooms were so small already, this might not have been practical. Besides, materials like these would long since have rotted away, so we cannot tell if they were used.

It is probable that such homes belonged to people of low **status**. Few or no slaves would have lived there – and the womenfolk would not have *needed* separate quarters because they spent much of their time doing **menial** jobs outside the home, to supplement the family income. Poor women might work in the fields or as servants or nurses – and enjoyed a good deal more freedom than wealthier females, even if they were not then seen to be so 'respectable'.

Bigger, more elaborate homes are attractive to **archaeologists** because they often contained wall paintings, mosaics or beautiful decorated pottery. Large numbers of them have been excavated, so it is tempting to believe that these were 'typical' ancient Greek homes. However, *more* typical homes – of a far cruder and simpler sort – are almost invisible to us today because they were not built to last.

Plato on the poor

According to the **philosopher** Plato, every Greek *polis* was in fact two separate city-states – one was made up of the rich, the other of the poor. Each had its own way of life, its own values – and each was naturally hostile to the other. There was a clear physical difference between men of different status too. Poor men were lean and sunburned, from having to work so hard out of doors in the hot Greek climate. The rich were pale and flabby. Plato believed that if, in time of war, poor men found themselves fighting alongside the rich, they would despise them and demand equality.

Organizing the home

Women spent much of their time organizing the household and supervising slaves in their daily duties.

'"Did you," asked Socrates, "teach your wife everything which relates to the management of a house?"
"I did," replied Ischomachus, "but not before I had implored the assistance of the gods, to show me what instructions were necessary for her."'

Suitable domestic spaces

Xenophon wrote the paragraph above. It gives an idea of the different roles of men and women in the ancient-Greek household. Ischomachus, a man of some wealth, went on to describe what he taught his wife. Here is what he said about the layout of his house, which helps to fill in the picture already sketched out for us by the discoveries of **archaeologists**:

'She first learned what a house was properly designed for; that it was not ordained to be filled with curious paintings or carvings, or such unnecessary decorations; but that the house should be built with due consideration, and for the convenience of its inhabitants … The most private and strongest room in the house seems to demand that money, jewels and other things that are rich and valuable should be placed there; the dry places expect corn; the cooler parts are most convenient for the wine; and the more **lightsome** and airy parts of the house for such things as require such a situation.

'I showed her which were the most convenient places for parlours and dining-rooms, that they might be cool in summer and warm in winter; and also, that as the front of the house stood to the south, it had the advantage of the winter's sun, and in the summer it rejoiced more in the shade. Then I appointed the bedchambers, and the nursery, and apartments for the women, divided from the men's lodging.' On the next page, you can read more about this division of the home between the sexes.

The house as a hive

Ischomachus bossed his wife around, but as mistress of the household, he said, she was like a 'Queen Bee'. 'She stays always in the hive, taking care that all the bees … are duly employed in their occupations; and those whose business lies outside the home, she sends out to do their duties. These bees, when they bring home their burdens, she receives, and instructs them to store their harvest till the time comes to use it. Then she shares it out fairly among those of her colony. She employs the bees who stay at home in **disposing** and ordering the combs … and likewise takes care of the young bees, seeing that they are well nourished and educated until they are able to go out and work for their living.' (The young bees here would have been children and possibly other relatives.)

The zone of Hestia

The Greek way of looking at the world was different from ours. They tended to see everything as divided into opposites: Greeks and **barbarians**; **citizens** and aliens; free men and slaves; male and female. To their minds, no bridges could be built between these opposites. They were too different.

There were also opposing zones within the ***polis***, watched over by particular **deities**. In cities there were two very carefully defined zones. One was that of the goddess Hestia, centred on hearth and home, the other was that of Hermes, god of the threshold and of the paths which led away from it. In other words, there was a 'female' indoor zone and an outdoor 'male' zone. While men went out and made their way in the world, women were supposed to stay at home as the 'trusty guardians of what's inside', according to the Athenian writer Apollodorus.

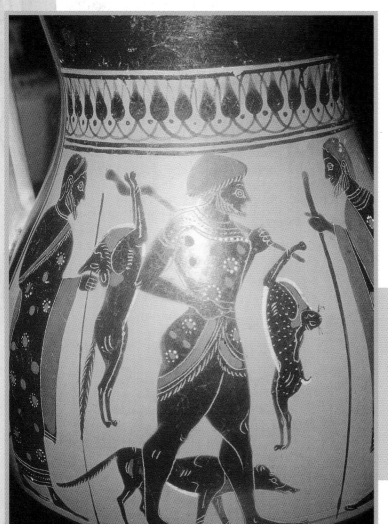

Bringing home the bacon – or its equivalent in ancient Greece! While women stayed at home in the zone of Hestia, the men went out to work and to hunt, to provide for their families.

Gunaikon and *andron*

Historians now argue over just how housebound most women were. It does seem that richer women, at least, were seldom seen in public. They were expected to supervise the running of their households (as Xenophon wrote, comparing the woman of the house to a Queen Bee: 'she stays always in the hive'), and work at textile crafts and entertain friends – all under their own roofs.

There could even be 'opposed areas' within the home itself. Since women spent more time there, their area – the *gunaikon* – was usually the larger. These were the parts of the house where they cooked, did their weaving and spinning, looked after children, and sometimes even slept – away from their husbands.

This vase image, from the 4th century BC shows a seated woman attended by a maid who would have helped to run her household.

Overstepping the mark

Several ancient writers made it clear that there were strictly divided men's and women's zones in some Greek houses. One of them was Lysias, in this passage: 'A man came to my house at night in a drunken state, broke down the doors, and entered the women's rooms. Inside were my sister and my nieces who had lived such well-ordered lives that they were embarrassed to be seen even by their relatives. This man, then, carried insolence to such a pitch that he refused to go away until the people who appeared on the spot and those who had accompanied him carried him off by force.' Clearly the intruder was not respecting the women's privacy and could only expect to be thrown out.

The *andron*

In Classical Athens, women seem to have kept to a house's more private rooms while the men used its public spaces. In larger homes, women's **quarters** were located well away from the street entrance, which was guarded by a male slave. In smaller homes, women might work and relax on an upper storey. We do not know how strictly separated the sexes were within the household, or for how much of the time.

Greek men reclining on their couches at a party in a luxurious-looking *andron*. The guests ate any food with knives, spoons and fingers. Entertainment is being provided by the standing musician.

From the 5th century BC, Greek writers mentioned that one room in the 'male' part of the house was elaborately decorated. This was known as the *andron* – from the Greek word for man, which was *aner*. (The word for woman was *gune*, from which we get *gunaikon*, or women's quarters.) When **archaeologists** examine an ancient-Greek home, this room is quite easy to identify.

The showpiece room

The *andron* was a small, almost square space. Its doorway was off-centre, to allow long couches to be placed along the wall next to it. This was the room where men gave banquets or parties. Often, since it was a place for guests, the *andron* was close to the main entrance, so it might therefore have windows opening on to the street. When it was not being used for entertainment, it is possible that the whole family used it too.

Some *androns* have been found with floors of pebble-**mosaic**. According to writers, some were decorated with **frescoes** and tapestries, or big cups were hung from the walls. There might also be round pictures called *tondos*. These showed amusing or shocking scenes and were kept turned to the wall, for a guest to take a peek at if he was curious.

The *symposium*

In Classical times (from about 500 to 300 BC), the best-known activity that took place in the *andron* was an all-male party called a *symposium*. In an earlier age, a great deal of fine Greek poetry, music and pottery was created for these events, which took a similar form all over the Greek world. (At rich men's houses, silver would probably have been used instead of pottery.) Nowadays a 'symposium' means a gathering of usually highly educated people – male and female alike – to discuss matters of common interest. In ancient Greece it was not always so intellectual!

Symposium etiquette

Since there might be as few as three couches in the *andron*, the groups could be quite small. In the room stood a large mixing-bowl or *krater*, in which wine was mixed with water, then poured by young male or female slaves into fine cups. Poetry and music were still performed, and the men would speak in turn on a chosen theme.

Plato's *symposium*

Sometimes at a *symposium* the guests would entertain each other by singing along to a **lyre**, telling jokes and riddles, reciting verses – or having serious discussions about important topics. The great thinker Plato wrote an account of one such discussion – called *The Symposium*. In it, brilliant Athenians like Socrates and Aristophanes debated the nature of love. The modern meaning of the word 'symposium' comes from this piece of writing.

This young man is carrying a couch as a three-legged table to be used at a *symposium*.

In his play *Wasps*, Aristophanes showed two men having this discussion:
'- Come and lie down, and learn how to behave at *symposia* and parties.
- How do I do it, then? Come on, tell me.
- Elegantly.
- You mean like this?
- Oh, *no*.
- How then?
- Straighten your knees and pour yourself over the cushions, flowing like an athlete. Then praise one of the bronzes, inspect the ceiling, admire the hangings in the hall.'
(This tells us that the walls of the *andron* could be covered with tapestries.)

A scene from an all-male *symposium*, dating from c.460 BC. The standing figure is a young cup-bearer, trained to mix and serve the wine during the evening.

Directing your dregs
The ancient Greeks seemed obsessed with the game of *kottabos*. Parents even hired tutors to teach its finer points to their children. Players had to leave some drops of wine in their cups, then take turns to flick these dregs at a small target called the *plastinx*, which stood on a *kottabos* stand, which itself stood on a narrow column at the end of the room. When the target was hit, a small tray fell off the stand with a clatter – along with a small figure called a *manos kottabos*. Bets were placed on the results of contests and, at organized competitions, the winner might receive anything from a valuable silver dish to a kiss.

Kitchen quarters

Although men might go to market to buy or order fresh food, women had the job of cooking it. When the sites of ancient homes are **excavated**, it is sometimes hard to tell exactly where the kitchen was. If bits of bone are found in certain parts of the flooring, along with deposits of ash, this may mean that once a kitchen with its oven stood on that spot. If bits of 'washroom' pottery (see next page) are found there too, it could mean that the same indoor fire was used both for cooking and for heating up bathwater.

A Greek woman cooks up a meal. Greek foodstuffs were believed to have particular 'powers' over the body – 'moistening', 'drying', 'heating', 'sweet', 'fatty' or 'strong'. A female cook was expected to combine them successfully.

In the homes of the rich, most kitchen work was done by female slaves. That gave their mistresses time to dream up exciting menus. The first cookery books came from Sicily – fragments from them show how popular fish dishes were. 'Cut off the head of the ribbon fish,' said one of the earliest surviving published recipes. 'Wash it and cut it into slices. Pour cheese and oil over it.'

Opson and sitos

Many Classical Greeks probably ate just one meal a day. This was the evening meal or *deipnon*. This did not consist of the two main elements of nourishment – food and drink – that we have today. The Greeks distinguished three. Like us, they had drink (usually wine diluted by water, or just water), which was taken *after* the food. Their food was divided into two elements: first the *sitos* or **staple**, which was usually bread made at home from grain, and second the *opson*, which was what you ate *on* the *sitos*. This could be almost anything else – olives, onions, garlic, fish – although meat was uncommon, except at feast-times when animals were sacrificed, cooked and eaten.

Different drinking practices

The Greeks were proud to be wine-drinkers – to them, only **barbarians** drank beer. In its raw form, Greek wine was sweet and strong, and usually had bits of grape and vine debris floating in it. So it had to be sieved before it was mixed with water then poured out. The Classical Athenians liked to drink socially in 'rounds' at their *symposia* (see page 30), passing cups around, with one toast after another. Spartans were more solitary drinkers – each man drinking from his own cup. This cup, called a *kothon*, could easily be carried in a soldier's kitbag. It had ridges to hold back any impurities in the water that Spartans had to drink when they were on the march.

Washing facilities

No Greek house had hot and cold running water. Water for drinking, cooking or washing had to be collected in large jars called *hydrias* from courtyard wells, or springs or fountains. Then, if necessary, it was heated over a naked flame. In hot and dusty ancient Greece it was easy to get dirty, but not many homes would have had special rooms set aside for bathing. Some were, however, discovered during the **excavations** at Olynthos.

These were part of three-room blocks consisting of a large living room, a small washroom and a **flue**, separated off at one end by a partition. This partition may have been open at the top, to let heat and smoke pass through. The flue may also have served as a kind of dump for domestic rubbish, since so much broken pottery was found there.

Clues from painted pottery

At other sites it is harder to tell where people washed – unless fragments of **terracotta** hipbaths are found in a certain place, or spaces for tubs are found in the cement. **Archaeologists** do sometimes find pottery vessels with 'bathroom scenes' painted on them and we now know that, in some cases, the Greeks decorated their pots with pictures of the activity that the pots were then used for. So, if a vessel showing people washing is found, there is a chance that long ago, on that very spot, Greek people actually washed themselves!

This image from a *hydria* shows a woman washing her hair at a basin that stands on a pedestal.

What do the washroom scenes show? Sometimes, there are women, clothed or unclothed, washing at a large basin called a *louterion*, which had a **pedestal**. There might be vessels nearby, called *amphorae* that were used for bringing water. Other scenes showed naked men washing in large basins, or scraping dead skin and dirt off their bodies with hand-tools called *strigils*.

This is a terracotta model of a woman in a bath, from the 5th century BC.

Home hygiene

In his play *Wasps* Aristophanes describes Philokleon coming home after he has served on a jury. He brings his small fee in his mouth – a common custom:

'Oh then what a welcome I get for its sake;

my daughter is foremost of all,

and she washes my feet and anoints them with care

and above them she stoops and lets a kiss fall

till at last by means of her pretty 'Papas'

she angles my three **obols** pay.'

This shows that washing another person's feet was a way of showing respect.

Home worship

'There is never equality between the race of deathless gods and that of men who walk the Earth.' Most ancient Greeks shared this view of Homer's. The Greeks saw things in opposites; **deities** and mortals were another example of this. Pindar wrote that although both races sprang from Mother Earth, they were 'kept apart by a difference in everything.' In a distant 'Golden Age', mortals and gods had used to dine together. Then, at the time of the first-ever sacrifice, the races were 'divided'. Every sacrifice after that time was a reminder of how wretched mankind was, and how blessed the **immortals** were. Human beings could now make their offerings to them only from a very great distance.

Household religion

At great religious festivals, **citizen**-priests made these sacrifices, hoping to win the gods' favour and support. There was no organized church with its own special officials, so when people wanted to worship in smaller groups, the most senior person present had to take charge. According to the **philosopher** Plato, all wise men were supposed to pray every morning and night – and the natural place to do this was in the home. Altars were set up in the courtyards of private homes, then the whole household worshipped together – with the head of the family supervising.

This woman may be about to pour an offering on an altar to a god. (The god himself may be the male figure pictured here.)

'The family that prays together, stays together.' A Greek family at prayer – with what may be a family pet!

Whereas the great festivals honoured the deities worshipped all over the Greek world (see box), individual households prayed to more local gods and goddesses, as well as to Zeus in his role as the defender of all family property: 'Zeus in the courtyard'. A family's father might also make sacrifices and seek blessings 'on behalf of' the whole household. Families might even go on small religious processions.

Greek religion was more to do with rituals than with inner **spirituality**. It focused on group activity, not on a person's private faith. However, every household, with its little statue of the god Hermes standing outside, felt that its survival and success depended upon a good relationship with the gods.

The family on Olympus

Zeus was the father-figure of a 'household' of the greatest Greek gods and goddesses that 'lived' on the summit of Mount Olympus in north-east Greece. Each of them was worshipped for particular purposes: Demeter for abundant crops, Pan for healthy flocks, Hephaestus was supposed to watch over blacksmiths, Prometheus over potters, and so on. When priests or heads of households made gifts to these gods through sacrifices, they prayed for special favours in return, using words like these: 'If ever I burnt the rich thighs of bulls and goats in your honour, grant me this prayer.'

Children in the home

'Plainly we look to wives who will produce the best children for us,' wrote Xenophon, 'and marry them to raise a family. The husband supports the wife who is to share in the production of his family, and provides in advance whatever he thinks the expected children will find useful in life.' When a baby boy was born into a Greek family, a crown of olive leaves was pinned to the front door of the house. This was a symbol of success, even 'victory'. When a girl was born, her family pinned some wool to the door. This symbolized the domestic work that she would do for the rest of her life.

It seems that few children, if any, had their own rooms in Greek houses. As infants they might have lived in the women's quarters, then they came to the more public rooms for special occasions. Maybe they played at times in the courtyard, and they certainly took part in family prayers there (see p37). We know what kinds of toys they played with from the paintings on vases, and also from 'grave goods'. These were items – like clay dolls, puppets, tops and rattles – that families buried with boys and girls who died young.

This is an ancient-Greek toy that has survived – a terracotta doll with jointed limbs.

Short childhoods

Poorer children had to help run the household from a very early age. In richer families, boys might go to school from the age of seven, while girls stayed home to learn practical skills. At around the age of thirteen girls were considered to be women. At a special ceremony they dedicated their toys to the goddess Artemis, before putting them away forever. To show they were grown-up they wore a girdle at their waists. When they got married, maybe only two years later, they dedicated the girdle to Artemis too.

Some children's toys have changed remarkably little since ancient times. The boy here is shown with a hoop. The man is holding a ball.

Greek gardens?

The diagram below shows the plan of a house built in the 4th century BC at Eretria, which was lived in for about a hundred years. It covered the large area of about 625 square metres, but probably had only a single storey. **Archaeologists** have called it the House of the **Mosaics**, since so many of the floors were decorated. This suggests that the owners were rich people. It is fascinating to take a look at this home, room by room, and try to imagine what might have happened in each of the inside spaces. As you will see, it may lead us to identify an unusual domestic space in ancient times – a garden.

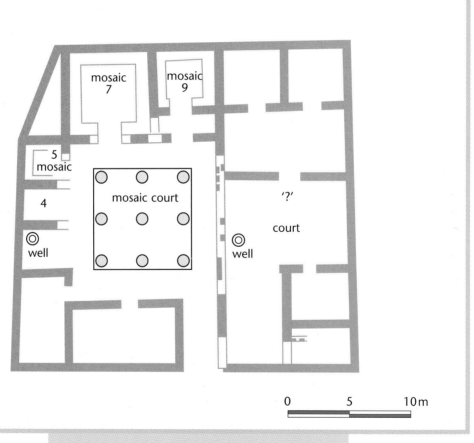

The plan of the House of Mosaics at Eretria. Was the area marked '?' a rare ancient-Greek garden? (see next page)

A guided tour

People entered the house from the south, and could go straight down a corridor into a central courtyard. Rooms 7 and 9 had raised benches for couches, so these were almost certainly the men's quarters. Room 5 may also have been an *andron* (see page 28), while the small room next to it (4) could have been a 'cloakroom' for guests. A marble table stood here, and there was a space for a large pottery vessel – which could have been a **chamberpot**! The neighbouring room had a well in it, so that may have been for washing hands.

A long wall separated the western section of the house from the eastern. There must once have been a door in it. Rooms in this eastern part were arranged around a *second* open area, which also included a water supply. It showed few signs of having been paved over like the western courtyard – and this led the **excavators** to deduce that it could have been a garden. If so, it was an unusual feature in an ancient-Greek home, at least until **Hellenistic** times (see box).

Most houses, especially in the cities, would not have been big enough to include a second courtyard. Most people, especially the poor, would not have had the time to cultivate a decorative garden. They relied on the plants grown in market gardens for their food.

Hellenistic gardens

In Hellenistic times, the rich became more interested in **conspicuous consumption** than in the Classical Age. Palm-trees were imported into Greece, and a letter survives from an official in Alexandria ordering his agent to plant 300 fir trees in the park on his **estate** – not just to supply timber for building ships, but also for the trees' 'striking appearance'. Ordinary people also admired trees and flowers.

How do we know?

The landscape of Greece is still littered with ruins from ancient times. Along with surviving Greek art and the work of Greek writers, this archaeological evidence often helps historians to form a clearer picture of the past. On page 16 you read about the important **excavations** that were made at Olynthos on the Chalkidiki peninsula. When the findings were published in 1940, one of the **archaeologists** claimed that it would become 'the main source of our evidence for the study of the Greek house.'

Secrets revealed by the site

A large number of homes could be studied at Olynthos. From this, the excavators discovered that there were a wide variety of house types in the city. Some of the dwellings were built to standard patterns, but it appeared that many had individual features, and were built to different **specifications**.

Olynthos looks like this today. Since no one has lived here since 348 BC, it has been relatively easy for archaeologists to excavate this ancient site.

There was no *direct* evidence that the houses were divided into male and female 'spaces'. However, in the light of ancient writings, the layouts do seem to suggest it. They also suggest that some members of the household – probably the women – were kept secluded from visitors. This can be deduced by the fact that there was usually only one door to each home. Access could therefore be controlled. Then, when an outsider entered, his (or her) movement inside could be 'channelled' so that at least some part of the house remained 'out of bounds'.

Yet no single site can ever tell the whole story. The findings at Olynthos must be set alongside discoveries made at many other sites. You have read about some of these in this book. Taken together, they reveal a number of secrets about domestic life in ancient Greece. There is still so much that we do not know about Greek homes – especially the homes of the poor – and how people lived in them. So there is still a great deal for archaeologists to find out for us!

Why *don't* we know?

Sparta was one of the greatest Greek city-states. Yet we must rely on written evidence for most of our information about it. Even in the 5th century BC, Thucydides, who wrote eight thrilling books about the **Peloponnesian** War, foresaw how little other evidence the Spartans would leave behind. He wrote: 'If the city of the Spartans were to become deserted and only the temples or the foundations of the buildings were left, I think that as time went by there would be few who would believe in Sparta's reputation – and yet it directly controls two-fifths of the Peloponnese, and dominates the rest and many cities outside it. It is not a co-ordinated city and has not got elaborate temples and buildings, but is formed of villages in the old Greek manner and would seem too insignificant.'

Timeline

All dates are BC

c.3000	Greece controlled till c.1450 by Minoan kings based on the island of Crete
c.1600–1100	Greek-speaking Mycenaeans rule separate kingdoms in mainland Greece
c.1100–800	Period of wars and migration
c.800–700	Homer's the *Iliad* and the *Odyssey* probably composed; Greece made up of small city states, ruled by separate kings or noble families
c.750–550	Greeks set up colonies in lands around Mediterranean
c.500	Some city-states become democracies; Athens the most powerful
c.490–479	Main period of **Persian** invasions of Greece
431–404	**Peloponnesian** War between Greek city-states, ending with Sparta eclipsing Athens as the most powerful state in mainland Greece
378–371	Sparta eclipsed by a new power – Thebes
336	Greece ruled until 323 by Alexander the Great of Macedon after conquest and invasion
146	Greece becomes part of the Roman Empire

Sources

Classical Greece
Ed. Roger Osborne
(Oxford University Press, 2000)

Eat, drink and be merry
Audrey Briers
(Ashmolean Museum, 1990)

Europe – a history
Norman Davies
(Oxford University Press, 1996)

Greece and the Hellenistic World
Ed. John Boardman, Jasper Griffin and Oswyn Murray
(Oxford University Press, 1988)

The Greeks
Paul Cartledge
(Oxford University Press, 1993)

House and society in the ancient Greek World
Lisa C. Nevett
(Cambridge University Press, 1999)

Political and social life in the Great Age of Athens
Ed. John Ferguson and Kitty Chisholm
(Ward Lock, 1978)

These were the Greeks
H.D. Amos and A.G.P Lang
(Hulton, 1979)

Glossary

archaeologists people who learn about the past by studying old buildings and objects

barbarians word used by ancient Greeks to describe anyone who was not Greek

barracks buildings where soldiers live

brazier pan or stand for holding lighted coals

chamberpot potty

citizen people in democracies who are allowed to vote

civilization way of life common to particular groups of people

colonnades linked series of columns

conspicuous consumption the spending of money on visible goods

consumer durables goods that do not wear out or get used up at once

deities gods and goddesses

disposing arranging

drachmas unit of Greek money, worth six *obols*

economic (in this sense) made for financial reasons

estate all the property of a person, usually someone wealthy

excavated dug up and examined by archaeologists

flue channel or passage, often for transmitting heat

frescoes water-colour paintings, laid on a wall or ceiling before the plaster dries

heir person, usually a relative, who inherits wealth or property

Hellenistic Greek-influenced, in the Greek style (*Hellen* was the Greek word for 'a Greek')

immortals creatures, unlike human mortals, who live forever

inscriptions words written on stone or a monument or a coin

lightsome full of light

lyre small, harp-like musical instrument

menial low-grade

metic foreigner, with some citizen's rights, living in a Greek city

mosaic design or picture made of small pieces of coloured stone, glass or clay

obol small Greek silver coin – six to a *drachma*

party walls walls shared by neighbours

pedestal base supporting a column, pillar or other object

Peloponnese region of southern Greece, including Sparta (see map on page 5)

peristyle row of columns surrounding a temple or courtyard, or the space that it encloses

Persian person who lived in the ancient Middle-Eastern kingdom of Persia, now known as Iran

philosopher seeker after wisdom, and often a teacher of great knowledge

polis Greek word for city-state

portico roof supported by columns at regular intervals

quarters own places

servile like a slave, over-respectful

society the whole community

specifications instructions

spirituality higher feelings of a holy sort

staple basic kind of foodstuff

status position in society

status symbols personal belongings that show someone's status

stucco plaster or cement used to coat wall surfaces

tenement building containing several dwellings

terracotta unglazed, usually brownish-red fine pottery

urban relating to a town or city (not to the countryside)

vaults series of arches that support a roof

ventilation system for letting air move about freely

Index